It's Catching

Warts and Verrucas

Angela Royston

www.heinemann.co.uk

Visit our website to find out more information about **Heinemann Library** books.

To order:

☎ Phone 44 (0) 1865 888066

▤ Send a fax to 44 (0) 1865 314091

▢ Visit the Heinemann Bookshop at www.heinemann.co.uk to browse our catalogue and order online.

First published in Great Britain by Heinemann Library,
Halley Court, Jordan Hill, Oxford OX2 8EJ
a division of Reed Educational and Professional Publishing Ltd.
Heinemann is a registered trademark of Reed Educational & Professional Publishing Ltd.

OXFORD MELBOURNE AUCKLAND JOHANNESBURG BLANTYRE
GABORONE IBADAN PORTSMOUTH (NH) USA CHICAGO

Designed by David Oakley/Arnos Design
Originated by Dot Gradations
Printed in Hong Kong/China

ISBN 0 431 12854 5
05 04 03 02 01
10 9 8 7 6 5 4 3 2 1

British Library Cataloguing in Publication Data
Royston, Angela
  Warts and verrucas. – (It's catching)
  1. Warts
  I. Title
  616.5'44

Acknowledgements

The Publishers would like to thank the following for permission to reproduce photographs:
Bubbles (Ian West) p13, Corbis (The Purcell Team) p12, Gareth Boden pp6, 17, 18, 20, 23, Images colour library p27, Martin Soukias pp4, 5, 19, 22, 24, 25, Powerstock (Zefa) p26, Robert Harding p10, Sally and Richard Greenhill p21, Science Photo Library pp7 (Quest), 8 (Sinclair Stammers), 9 (Clinique Ste Catherine), 11 (Mark Clarke), 14(P Marazzi), 15 (P Marazzi), 16 (P Marazzi), Stone (Amwell) p29, Telegraph colour library p28.

Cover photograph reproduced with permission of Science Photo Library.

Every effort has been made to contact copyright holders of any material reproduced in this book. Any omissions will be rectified in subsequent printings if notice is given to the Publisher.

Any words appearing in bold, **like this**, are explained in the glossary.

Contents

What are warts and verrucas?

Warts are small bumps in the skin on your face or hands caused by a **virus**. Verrucas are warts that affect the skin on the soles of your feet.

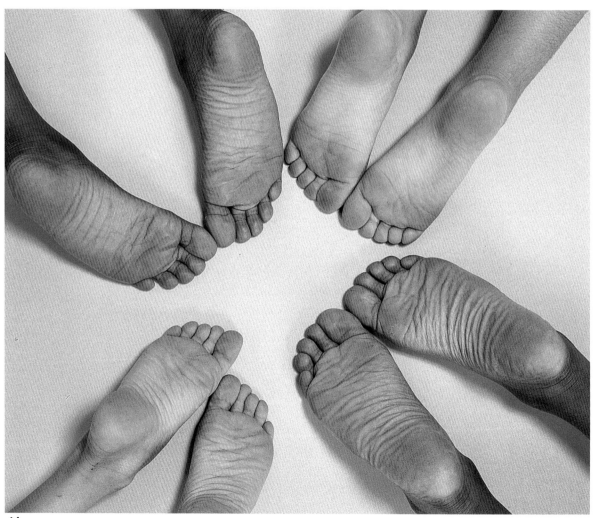

Verrucas and warts are not serious, but they can be uncomfortable. This book looks at what causes them, how they are spread and how they can be treated.

Healthy skin

Skin covers your whole body like a stretchy wrapper. It stops dirt, **germs** and other harmful things getting inside your body.

The outer layer of skin is made of tiny, hard flakes. This is what skin looks like under a **microscope**.

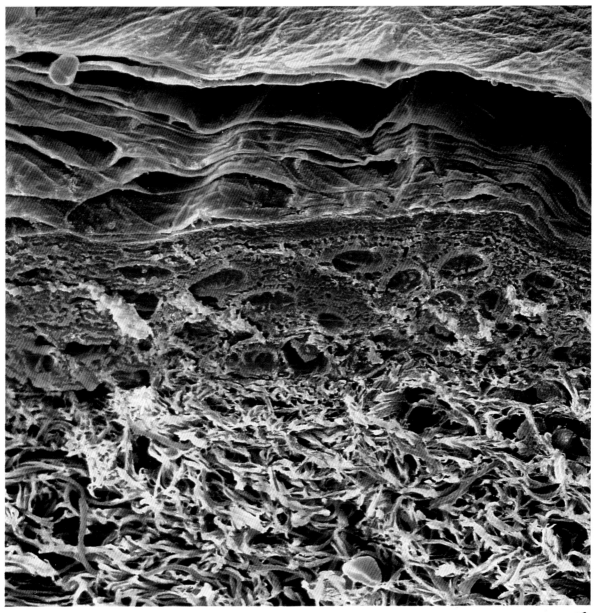

What causes illness?

Many illnesses are caused by **germs**, called **bacteria** or **viruses**. Germs are so small they can only be seen through a powerful **microscope**.

This is the virus that causes warts and verrucas. Each wart contains millions of wart viruses. They can be passed from one person to another.

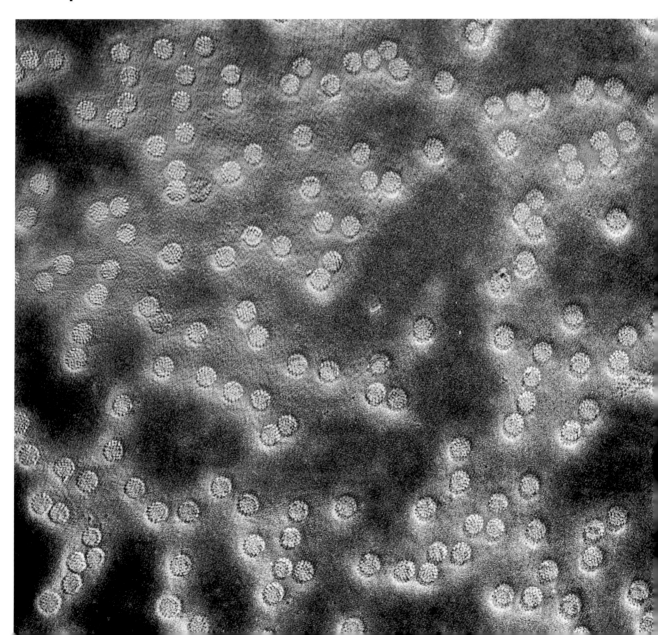

How do you catch warts?

When an illness can be passed from one person to another, we say it is catching or **infectious**. To catch warts, you have to touch the **virus**.

The virus gets into the body through cuts or breaks in the outer layer of the skin. It is important to keep cuts clean and covered up as much as you can.

Catching verrucas

Warts on the hands and face are not very **infectious**. You can catch verrucas more easily. You catch them by walking on the **virus** in bare feet.

Be careful! If you touch your own wart or verruca you can spread it to another part of your skin.

What do warts look like?

Warts may be rough or smooth. Sometimes the skin around them goes a bit darker than the rest of the skin. Most are not sore.

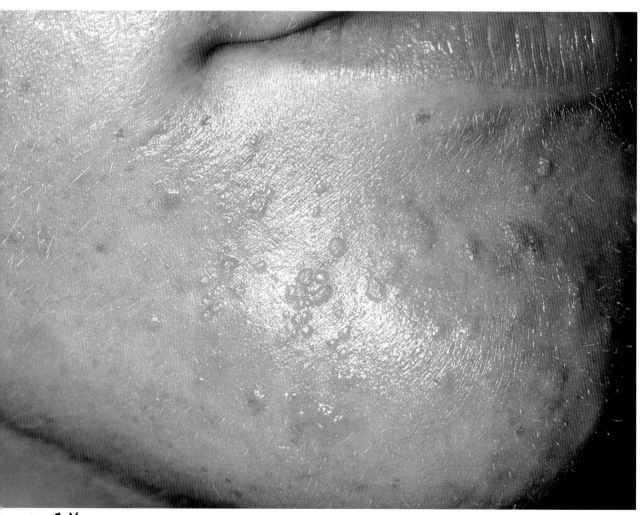

Warts may take months before they appear. They will eventually go away on their own as your body kills the **virus**.

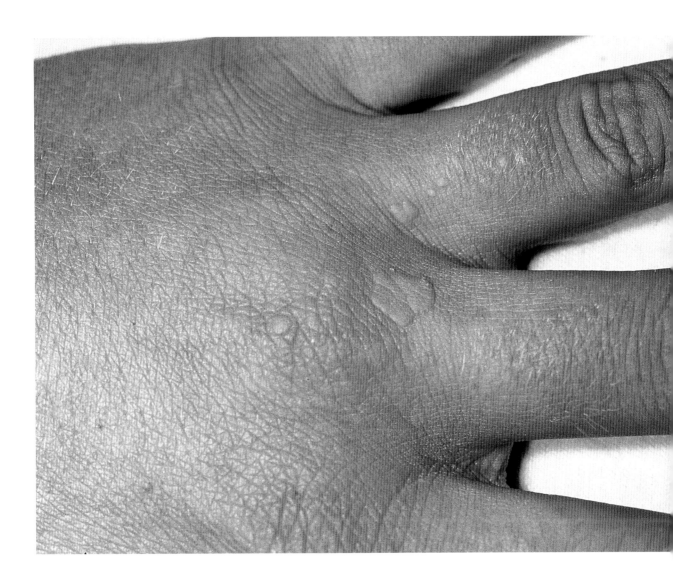

What do verrucas look like?

Warts on your feet are called verrucas or plantar warts. Verrucas usually have a black spot in the middle.

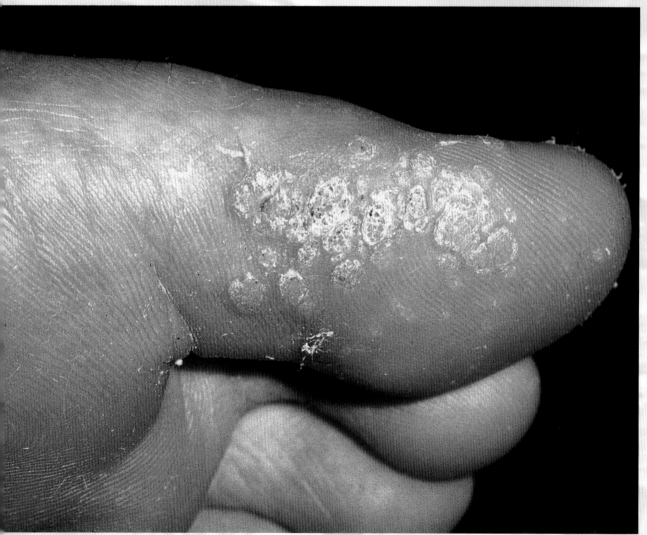

If you do not treat a verruca, you may soon have several more. Some large verrucas go deep into the skin and are very painful to walk on.

Treatment

Chemists sell many different **ointments** for treating warts and verrucas. The ointment is rubbed on to the wart. Follow the instructions carefully.

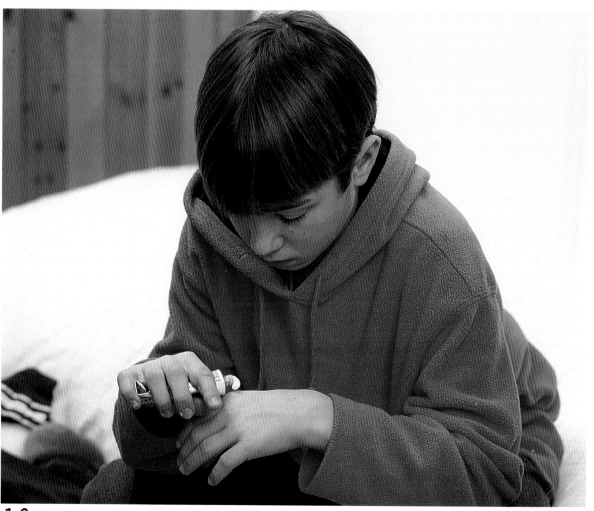

The wart may have to be covered with a **plaster**. The ointment slowly kills the skin around the wart, but it may take several weeks to work.

Other treatments

Some **herbal remedies** are gentler than **ointments**. Ask an adult if you want to try to find one that works.

Some warts and verrucas are hard to get rid of! Then a doctor may decide to **freeze** the wart off or use a **laser** to remove it.

How to avoid warts

If you want to avoid warts and verrucas, wash your feet and hands regularly. Don't suck pens or your thumb and don't use anyone else's towel. Shower before you swim.

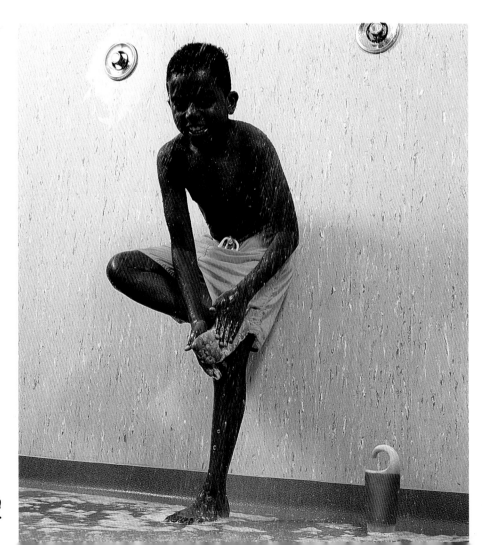

Remember, wart **viruses** can only affect you if the skin is broken. Cover up cuts and **grazes** to keep the virus out.

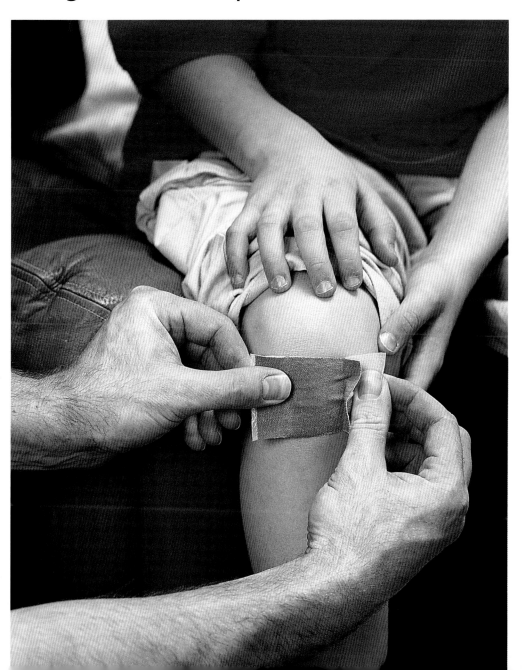

Don't spread warts!

If you have warts or verrucas, don't let other people borrow your towel. Don't let them wear your gloves or flip-flops.

Don't run around in bare feet if you have a verruca. You can still go swimming, but you must wear a **verruca sock**.

Well and healthy

If you are healthy, you are less likely to get ill. Eating plenty of fruit and raw vegetables helps your body fight and kill **viruses**.

Taking exercise and keeping clean also helps you to stay well and healthy. Change your socks often and don't wear dirty clothes.

Think about it!

Suppose that one of these children has warts on his hands. How might the wart **viruses** spread from one child to another?*

If one of these children has verrucas, how can that child stop the other children catching them?*

*Answers on page 30.

Answers

Page 28

Some of the wart **viruses** might rub off on to the ball. When the other children catch the ball, some of the viruses will stick to their hands. If there is a break in the skin on any of their hands, the virus may infect them.

Page 29

If one of the children has verrucas, they should wear a **verruca sock** on the infected foot. You should always shower before and after swimming whether you have verrucas or not.

Stay healthy and safe!

1 Always tell an adult if you feel ill or think there is something wrong with you.
2 Never take any **medicine** or use any **ointment** or lotion unless it is given to you by an adult you trust.
3 Remember, the best way to stay healthy and safe is to eat good food, to drink plenty of water, to keep clean and to wear the correct clothes.

Glossary

bacteria   tiny living things – most bacteria are harmless, but some can make you ill if they get inside your body

chemists   people who sell medicines and things that you usually use in the bathroom

freeze   make very cold – when living things, such as viruses, become very cold they die

germs   tiny living things that can make you ill if they get inside your body

graze   scrape

herbal remedy   medicine made from plants

infectious   something, especially an illness, that can be passed from one person to another

laser   very narrow beam of strong light – doctors use lasers to burn or cut parts of the body

medicine   substance used to treat or prevent an illness

microscope   something that makes very small things look big enough to see them

ointment   oily cream that often contains medicine and is rubbed into the skin

plaster   piece of sticky material, usually with a pad of soft cloth, used to cover part of the skin

verruca sock   special waterproof sock that swimmers use to cover a verruca

virus   tiny things that can make you ill if they get inside your body

Index

Titles in the *It's Catching* series include:

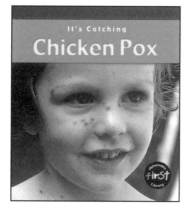

Hardback   0 431 12850 2

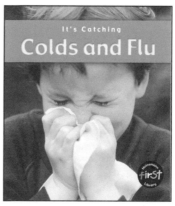

Hardback   0 431 12851 0

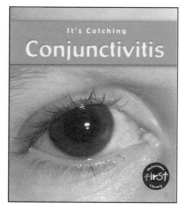

Hardback   0 431 12852 9

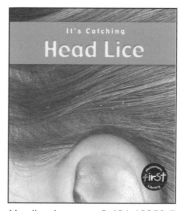

Hardback   0 431 12853 7

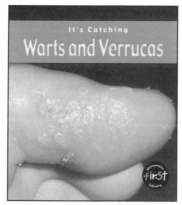

Hardback   0 431 12854 5

Find out about the other titles in this series on our website www.heinemann.co.uk/library